W9-BXM-792

DRAWING

Hilary Devonshire

Consultant: Henry Pluckrose

Photography: Chris Fairclough

FRANKLIN WATTS
New York/London/Sydney/Toronto

Copyright © 1990 Franklin Watts

Franklin Watts
387 Park Avenue South
New York
NY 10016

Design: Edward Kinsey
Editor: Jenny Wood
Typeset by Lineage Ltd,
Watford, England
Printed in Belgium

Acknowledgement
The author wishes to record her thanks in the preparation of this book to: Henry Pluckrose for his advice and guidance; Christopher Fairclough for the excellence of his step-by-step photographs; and Chester Fisher, Franklin Watts Ltd.

The following photographs are reproduced by permission of the Electricity Council: 12 on page 22, 13 on page 22 and 3 on page 25.

The following photographs were taken by Henry Pluckrose: 5 on page 8, 6 on page 8, 6 on page 13, 16 on page 24 and 8 on page 28.

Library of Congress Cataloguing-in-Publication Data
Devonshire, Hilary.
    Drawing / Hilary Devonshire.
       p.   cm.—(Fresh start)
    Includes index.
    Summary: An introduction, in text and photographs, to drawing techniques and the range of materials used to produce a variety of textures and effects.
    ISBN 0-531-10757-4
    1. Drawing—Technique—Juvenile literature.   2. Artists' materials—Juvenile literature.   3. Texture (Art)—Juvenile literature.   [1. Drawing—Technique.   2. Artists' materials. 3. Texture (Art)]   I. Title.   II. Series: Fresh start (London, England)
    NC730.D47   1990
    741.2—dc20   89-36496
                                                                      CIP
                                                                      AC

Contents

This book describes activities which use the following:

Apron (or old shirt)
Burlap (small piece)
Candles (white)
Cardboard
Chalks
Charcoal
Cold water dyes
Crayons
Eraser (soft rubber)
Fixative
Glue
Graphite
Inks — drawing inks
    — waterproof ink
Knife
Knitting needle
Magazine
Modeling clay
Natural objects (e.g. an apple, a flower, a leaf)
Newspaper
Paintbrush
Paints — poster colors
    — watercolors

Paper — cartridge paper
    — sketch pads
    — construction paper
    — typing paper
Paper doily
Pastels — chalk pastels
    — oil pastels
    — soft pastels
Pencil sharpener
Pencils (varying grades)
Pens — cartridge pens
    — felt-tip pens
    — fiber-tip pens
    — fountain pens
Printing roller
Ruler
Saucer (old)
Scissors
Sponge (small piece)
Stick (thin)
Scotch tape
Tissues
Water, and water jar
Water soluble colors — crayons
    — pastels
    — pencils

Drawing is the art of creating a picture or design by making lines on a surface with a pen, pencil, or other mark-making instrument. Having a variety of crayons, pencils and sheets of paper in front of you, all ready to use, is exciting. It encourages you to want to make a picture.

What will you draw? To develop your skill, you need to practice drawing different sorts of subjects – buildings, people, landscapes, or things from nature such as animals, birds and plants. You may want to try quick sketches, or you may prefer to work slowly and carefully, studying your subject in detail.

Some hints

Keep your pencils, pencil sharpener and erasers in a pencil case or jar. Other drawing materials such as crayons, charcoals, inks and pens, can be stored in a large box.

Remember that there are many types of paper. Some are smooth and shiny, others have rougher surfaces. As you work, you will discover how each type can create a different effect.

For some of the later activities in this book where you work with inks or paint, you will need an apron or old shirt to protect your clothes. When you work "wet" you will also need to cover your working surface with newspaper or a plastic sheet.

This book is designed to encourage you to explore the art of drawing. It suggests ways in which you can experiment with a range of materials, for it is through exploration that you will come to understand how the various materials and equipment behave. I hope, too, that as you work through the ideas, you will discover the delights and pleasures of drawing.

Wax crayons are fun to work with. They are made in a wide range of sizes and colors. They can be sharpened to a point for line work or used flat on their side to give broad strokes.

You will need different colored wax crayons and a selection of paper.

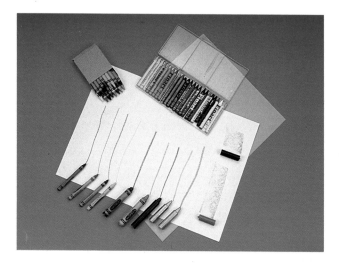

1 Different crayons give different effects.

Try to make a picture using only lines. You can make a fine line by pressing lightly, or you can press hard for strong, heavy color. Experiment with just one colored crayon on colored paper.

2 Draw a picture in lines, using a thin crayon.

3 Add further lines in different colors to complete the design. Notice that the picture is made up of lines only. It has not been colored in.

4 *The Discovery* A white line drawing on a blue background.

Careful observation can develop your sense of distance. The art of drawing a picture so that you give an impression of distance is called perspective.

5 Church Interior

6 Village Street

You will need a selection of pencils, paper, an eraser, and a pencil sharpener or knife.

Pencils are graded according to the hardness or softness of the graphite they contain. The most common is the medium grade HB. Softer pencils are graded from B to 7B (the softest), and harder pencils from H to 7H (the hardest). You can buy pencils in a wide range of colors.

Rough, grainy papers, such as watercolor paper, provide a good surface for pencil work. Smooth papers can be used for the softer leads. Sketch pads are useful for outdoors and for making a collection of sketches.

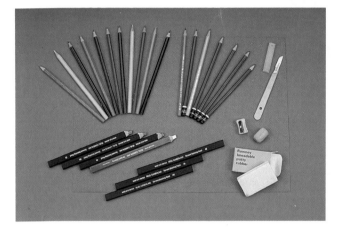

1 Equipment for drawing with pencils.

2 A selection of papers for drawing. Notice that sketch pads are included.

When you draw, always start with a sharp pencil. Pencil sharpeners are safe and easy to use, but pencils sharpened with a knife give a longer point and therefore stay sharper for a greater length of time.

3 Make a stroke with each of your pencils, to test their grades. Does pressing harder make a difference? The flat pencils here are grades B, 2B and 4B.

4 Experiment with a flat pencil to make different shapes and patterns.

Tones are different shades of gray and black. You can make tones with lines, dots and other patterns. Crossed lines are called cross-hatching. Different tones made in this way can be used in pencil drawing as a means of shading the darker areas.

You will need a selection of pencils and paper.

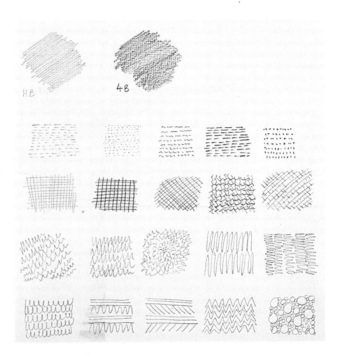

1 Examples of tones. Make a collection of your own. Experiment with different grades of pencil.

Scribbles, strokes and spirals drawn quickly in freehand can give depth to a flat drawing.

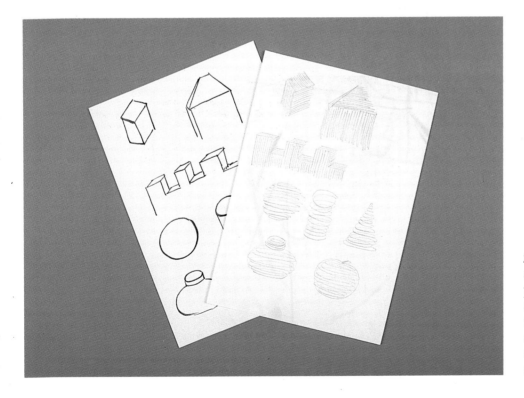

2 Draw some flat shapes on a piece of paper. Place another sheet of thin paper on top. Try to give the shapes body and depth using scribbles, strokes and spirals.

3 *Church* Make a quick sketch using a broad, soft pencil such as a flat 4B.

4 Now make a second picture using a sharply pointed pencil such as an ordinary HB to give finer detail.

5 Here, quick strokes and spirals create a good impression of a battle scene.

6 A head drawn in soft pencil. Can you work out how the different tones have been achieved?

Object drawing

A way of developing your skills is to arrange, then draw, one or more objects. Look at your arrangement very carefully before you begin.

7 This sketch was done with a graphite pencil followed by colored pencils. You could use a flashlight to change the direction of the light and therefore the position of the shadows.

8 *Soldiers* A sketch made using colored pencils.

A frame made from cardboard can be used like the viewfinder in a camera to help you choose what you want to draw and how you want to draw it. Should your picture be a wide, horizontal shape? (This is known as a *landscape* layout.) Perhaps it would look better as a tall, vertical picture, a *portrait* layout? How much of your subject do you want to show in the picture?

You will need cardboard, a pencil, a ruler, scissors, scotch tape, a stick and modeling clay.

1 A piece of cardboard with a square or rectangular hole makes a useful frame.

2 Keep your frame in position while you draw by taping it on to a stick held in modeling clay.

3 Two L-shaped pieces of cardboard will give many shapes and sizes when overlapped. Make small marks on the inside edges of each piece of cardboard, 1cm (½in) apart. These marks will act as guides when forming a frame.

4 Find a picture or photograph and use your L-shaped pieces of cardboard to help you choose a section which will be interesting to draw.

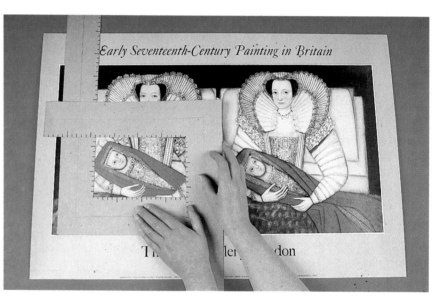

Early Seventeenth-Century Painting in Britain

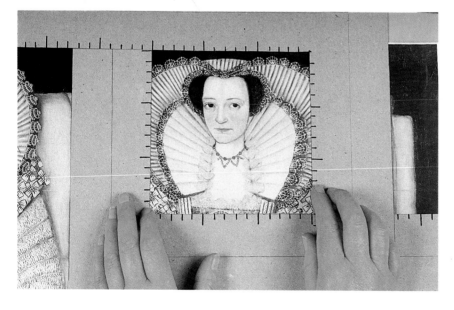

5 A square makes a good frame for this portrait detail.

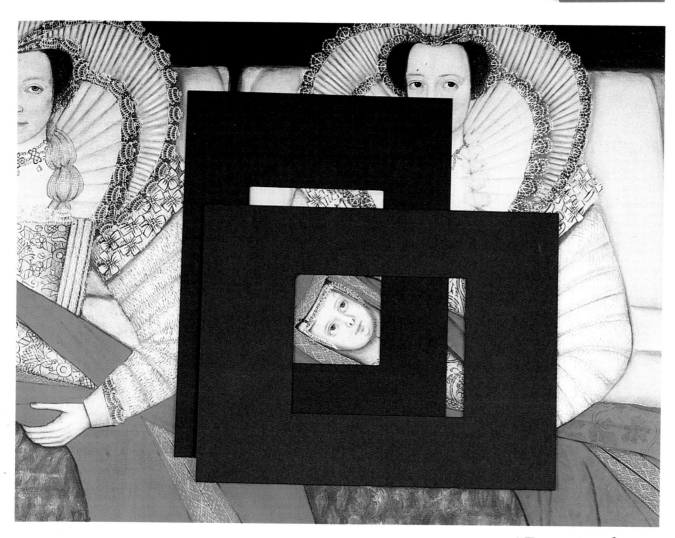

6 Two rectangular frames can also be used to select the detail you wish to copy.

Graphite, chalk and charcoal are all soft materials which blend easily. They can be textured with the fingers or lightened by using a kneaded eraser. This soft quality means that pictures worked in any of these materials need to be "fixed" to prevent smudging.

1 A selection of equipment for use when drawing with graphite, chalk and charcoal.

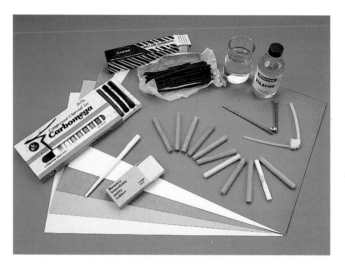

Drawing with graphite
Solid sticks of graphite are like pencils with no wooden casing.

You will need graphite sticks, paper, a paper doily and a knife.

2 A graphite stick on its side will give broad strokes. Use one in this way to take an impression of the paper doily. You could cut and tear your own paper shapes to create a background landscape for a drawing like this.

3 Use the knife to make some graphite powder.

4 Spread the powder with your fingers to start a picture.

5 *Volcano* Add lines to complete the picture.

Making a paper stump

When you are working with graphite, chalks or charcoal, a paper stump is a useful tool. It will prevent your fingers getting dirty and leaving smudgy prints on your picture.

You will need a strip of paper, a knitting needle and Scotchtape.

6 To make a paper stump, curl the strip of paper around the knitting needle.

7 Pull the knitting needle away and tighten one end of the stump to a point. Fasten the stump with tape so that it does not unroll.

Drawing with chalks

Chalks can be obtained in a range of colors. They smudge easily, and different colors can be blended by rubbing gently with your finger or with a paper stump. When your picture is finished, spray it with fixative to prevent smudging.

You will need a selection of chalks, paper, a paper stump, and fixative.

8 First draw your picture in chalk.

9 Using the paper stump, experiment with blending some of the colors.

10 Fix your design using fixative.

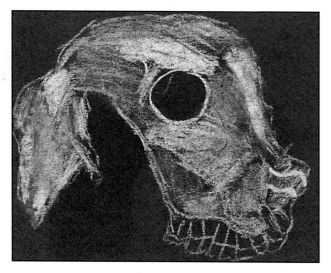

11 *Skull* White chalk is
effective on a black
background.

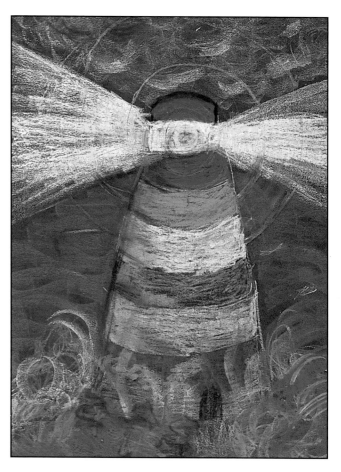

12 *Lighthouse* This
picture was made with
colored chalks on a
blue background.

13 *Iron* Can you find a
household object
which would be
interesting to draw?

Drawing with charcoal

Charcoal (charred wood) was the first drawing material used by humans. In prehistoric times it was used to draw the outlines of animals on cave walls.

Nowadays, sticks of charcoal are made by burning thin twigs slowly in special kilns.

As well as the common black charcoal, you can also buy charcoals in a range of grays.

You will need a selection of charcoal, paper, chalk and a paper stump.

14 Experiment with different shades of gray. If you do not have special gray charcoals, try blending your black charcoal with white chalk.

15 Using a charcoal stick, draw an outline of your picture. Color it with charcoal and chalk. Smudge some areas with the paper stump for special effect.

24

16 *Troll* The finished picture.

There are several different types of pastel. Some are chalky, others are soft and easy to handle. Oil pastels blend together easily. As you experiment with different pastels you will learn how they behave. Try working on tinted papers, or on paper with a rough, grainy surface such as Bristol board or watercolor paper.

You will need soft pastels, paper and a flower or leaf.

1 Using your soft pastels, lay down some areas of color side by side. Use four or five different colors and rub gently with your finger to blend them together.

2 Carefully copy the colors from the flower or leaf. Can you mix your pastels to the right shades?

3 *Drying My Hair* A selfportrait worked in pastel.

Camouflaging a square

This idea shows how versatile pastels can be. Every color can be created from one set of oil pastels if they are mixed together very carefully.

You will need oil pastels, a small piece of cardboard or a blank postcard, a pencil, a ruler, scissors, an old magazine, paper and glue.

4 First cut a hole 5cm square in the center of the piece of cardboard or postcard. Find a colored picture in the magazine and use your "viewfinder" frame (see page 15) to select an interesting section. Choose a section with a variety of colors around the edges.

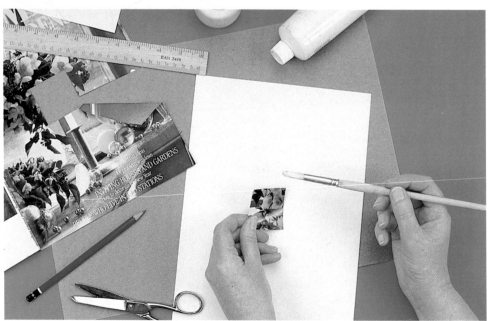

5 Cut out the picture section and paste it on to the center of a sheet of paper.

6 Using your oil pastels, work out from the edges of the picture section, trying to match the color tones exactly. You will need to work carefully to blend the right colors. Sometimes you may need to mix two or three colors together.

7 The finished picture. Can you see the camouflaged square?

8 *Crowd Scene* A
picture made with oil
pastels.

Long ago, monks used pens to write and illustrate their books. These pens were usually quill pens made from goose feathers, and the monks wrote on skins from sheep or goats.

Nowadays there are many types of pen: fountain pens and cartridge pens which hold their own ink, dip pens for use with bottles of ink, and many types of fiber- and felt-tip pens. The different pens vary greatly in size.

You will need to try out your pens to see if they give a broad, wide line, or a fine, narrow line.

Drawing inks are supplied in a range of colors. Some inks can be diluted with water. Some, such as Indian ink, are waterproof. When working with pens and inks, it is best to work on fairly strong, smooth paper.

You will need a selection of pens, inks and paper.

1 A selection of materials for drawing with pen and ink.

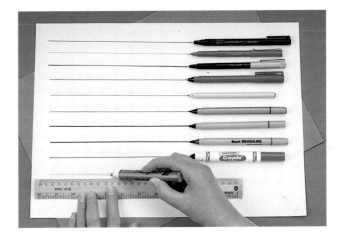

2 Make a collection of lines to test your pens. Which pens make a very fine line?

3 Try sketching with a fine tipped pen. You can vary the tones in your shading using dots, lines and cross-hatching, just as you did in your pencil sketches.

4 Try coloring a picture using only lines.

5 *Native Warrior* This was done by a 5-year-old, using a felt-tip pen.

6 *Falcon* A fiber-tip pen design. How many animals can you see?

7 *Into Battle* This too was drawn with felt-tip pens.

8 Monks often decorated the first letter of a new piece of text. You could choose a letter and try to decorate it.

It is possible to remove color
using special painting sticks.

1 Color a shape using
a special painting
stick.

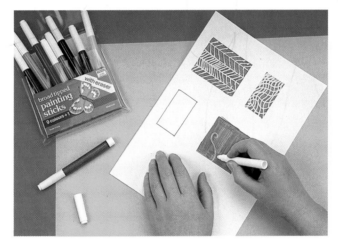

2 Draw a design using
the eraser stick.

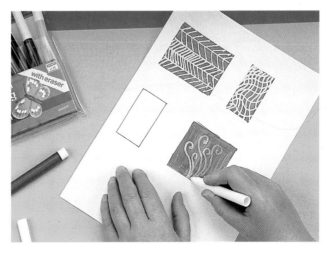

3 Your design will
slowly appear as the
color disappears.

4 *Portrait* The white lines and patterns were made by removing color.

There are a variety of water soluble pencils, crayons and pastels which are fun to use. They can be used both dry and wet, on rough or smooth papers.

You will need a selection of water soluble colors, paper, water and a paintbrush.

1 Some water soluble colors: water soluble pencils (top), painting crayons (center), painting pastels (bottom).

2 Test your colors to see how they blend together when you wet them with the paintbrush.

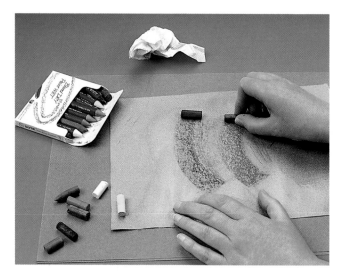

3 Try working on wet paper. Use a painting pastel on its side to prepare a background for a drawing.

4 Alternatively, color the background with pastels and soften the colors with a wet brush.

5 Draw a picture using a water soluble pencil, crayon or pastel dipped in water.

6 *Trees* The finished picture.

You will need waterproof ink, a pen or brush, paper, watercolor paints and a paintbrush.

1 Draw a picture on smooth paper using waterproof ink and the pen or brush.

2 *When the ink is dry, color your picture with watercolor paints. The ink can help to stop the colors running together.*

3 *Waterfront* The finished picture.

4 Here cold water dyes were used, and the colors allowed to blend together.

Many drawings are made more interesting by being worked on a textured background. You may, for example, like to tint your own paper using a watercolor wash. On a rough weave paper, using a pastel on its side gives an interesting effect.

You can also create different textures by *removing* color. Use different types of material to do this. Try making a sample sheet of the various effects you achieve.

You will need watercolor paints, a paintbrush, water, an old saucer, paper, tissues, a piece of burlap, a sponge and a printing roller.

1 Paint a small area of a sheet of paper with watercolor.

2 Remove some of the color by pressing down on it with a crumpled tissue. Make a print elsewhere on the paper with the paint-covered tissue.

3 Experiment using different materials to give you new textures. Here a piece of burlap and a sponge have been used.

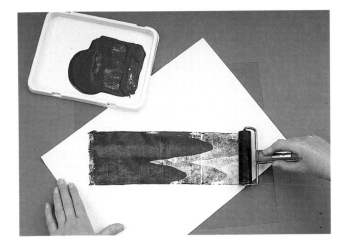

4 Use a printing roller to create a background.

5 Your background may give you an idea for a picture. Could you draw people on the blue mountains?

6 Working on a sponge-textured background.

On your own

Having used this book you will have experimented with a variety of techniques. You will have worked with many materials, and discovered how they behave with different types of papers and textured surfaces.

Here are a few more ideas for you to try. Have fun!

1 Make a picture which combines two or more of the ideas contained in this book. For example, you could draw with inks on a surface prepared with water soluble crayons. Or you could make a crayon drawing and wash over your picture with diluted ink.

1 *On The Farm* This picture was made using watercolors and felt-tip pens.

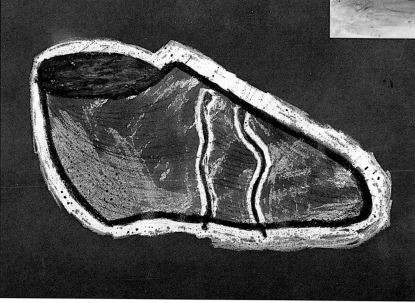

2 *Roman Shoe* This sketch of an object in a museum was done with wax crayons and a black ink wash.

2 Make a pencil sketch to use as a foundation for a painting. If you are sketching outdoors, make a note of the colors as you work.

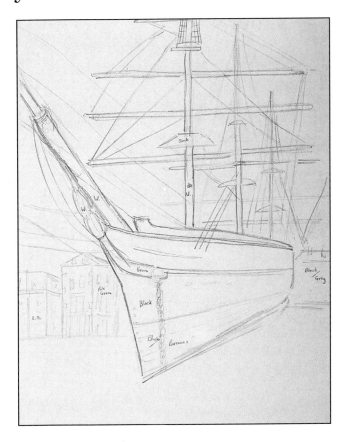

3 *The Cutty Sark* A pencil sketch.

4 The finished picture, using acrylic paints.

5 *My Bike* This effect was achieved by using poster paint over a pencil drawing.

Candle drawings

For this idea you need a white candle, paper, some colored drawing ink, an old saucer and a paintbrush.

6 Draw a picture with the wax candle.

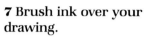

7 Brush ink over your drawing.

8 The wax of the candle resists the ink and your picture appears through the ink wash.

Drawing with hot candle wax
ASK AN ADULT TO HELP WITH THIS.

Make a drawing using melted candle wax which has been heated in an old saucepan. Work on a table covered with plenty of old newspaper, and be careful not to spill any wax. Use inks or cold water dyes to color your picture. When you have finished, remove the wax by ironing your picture through several sheets of newspaper.

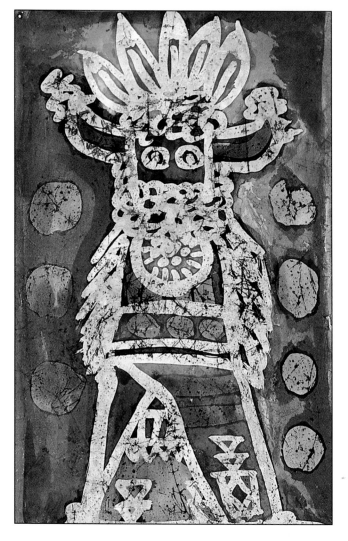

9 *Indian Chief* A candle wax drawing created from a museum sketch.

3 Make a book of sketches.

10 Your sketches could include illustrations for a story, copies of interesting objects in a museum, or scenes from a holiday.

Most of the materials mentioned in this book are easy to obtain. Most stationers stock a range of paper suitable for the activities described, as well as a selection of pencils, pens and inks.

Wax crayons

Good quality wax crayons are made in a wide range of thicknesses and colors. They are obtainable from arts and crafts stores as well as from good stationers.

Fixatives

Fixatives are available for protecting pictures that have been made with soft materials such as pastels and chalk. Most fixatives are available in a spray can. Alternatively, hair spray can be used, although it is best to experiment on a small sample of work first to make sure the spray does not cause discoloring.

Special artists' materials

Special materials such as graphite sticks, charcoal, broad pencils, pastels, inks and watercolors can be obtained from arts and crafts stores and some stationers.